WHY
ONE WAY?

WHY
ONE WAY?

*Defending an Exclusive Claim
in an Inclusive World*

BY

JOHN MACARTHUR

W PUBLISHING GROUP™

www.wpublishinggroup.com

A Division of Thomas Nelson, Inc.
www.ThomasNelson.com

ISBN 0-8499-5558-0

02 03 04 05 06 BVG 6 5 4 3 2 1

Contents

 *Introduction*

In the Jesus Movement of the 1960s and '70s, the "One Way" sign—the index finger held high—became a popular icon. "One Way" bumper stickers and lapel pins were everywhere, and the "One Way" slogan pretty much became the identifying catchphrase of all evangelicalism.

Evangelicalism in those days was an extremely diverse movement. (In some ways it was even more eclectic than it is today). It encompassed everything from Jesus People, who were an integral part of that era's youth culture, to straight-line fundamentalists, who scorned everything contemporary. But all of them had at least one important thing in common: They knew that Jesus Christ is the only way to heaven. "One Way" seemed an unshakable belief that all evangelicals shared in common.

That is no longer the case. The evangelical movement of today is no longer unified on this issue. Some who call themselves evangelicals are openly insisting that faith alone in Jesus is not the only way to heaven. They are now convinced that people of all faiths will be in heaven. Others are simply cowardly, embarrassed, or hesitant to affirm the exclusivity of the gospel in an era when inclusivity, pluralism, and tolerance are deemed supreme virtues by the secular world. They imagine it would be a tremendous cultural *faux pas* to declare that Christianity is *the* truth and all other faiths are wrong. Apparently, the evangelical movement's biggest fear today is that we will be seen as out of harmony with the world.

Why has this dramatic shift taken place? Why has evangelicalism abandoned what we once all agreed is absolutely true? I believe it is because church leaders, in their desperate quest to be relevant and fashionable, have actually failed to see where the contemporary world is going and why.

We're not living in the modern world anymore. This is the *postmodern* world. And postmodernism is just as hostile as modernism to the truth of Christianity—perhaps even more so. The philosophical issues are different, but the world's hostility to the truth of Scripture has not abated one bit.

Now is not the time to make friends with the world. It is certainly no time to capitulate to worldly cries for pluralism and inclusivism. Unless we recover our conviction that Christ is the *only* way to heaven, the evangelical movement will become increasingly weak and irrelevant.

It is ironic that so many who are downplaying the exclusivity of Christ are doing it because they believe it is a barrier to "relevance." Actually, Christianity is not relevant at all if it is merely one of many possible paths to God. The relevance of the gospel has always been its absolute exclusivity, summed up in the truth that Christ alone has atoned for sin and therefore Christ alone can provide reconciliation with God for those who believe only in Him.

The early church preached Christ crucified, knowing that the message was a stumblingblock to the religious Jews and foolishness to the philosophical Greeks (1 Corinthians 1:23). We need to recover that apostolic boldness. We need to remember that sinners are not won by clever public relations or the powers of earthly persuasion, but the gospel—an inherently exclusive message—is the power of God unto salvation.

This brief book is meant as a reminder of the gospel's distinctiveness. That very narrowness sets Christianity apart from every other worldview. After all, the whole point of Jesus' best-known sermon was to declare that the way to destruction is broad and well traveled, while the way of life is so narrow that few find it (Matthew 7:14). Our task as ambassadors of God is to point to that very narrow way. Christ Himself is the one way to God, and to obscure that fact is, in effect, to deny Christ and to disavow the gospel itself.

We must resist the tendency to be absorbed into the fads and fashions of worldly thought. We need to emphasize, not downplay, what makes Christianity unique. And in order to do that effectively, we need to have a better grasp of how worldly thought is threatening sound doctrine in the church. We must be able to point out just where the narrow way diverges from the broad way.

It is to that end that I offer this little book. It is just a brief overview, but my prayer is that it will help set the truth of the gospel in clear contrast to all the wisdom of this world. "Let no one deceive himself. If anyone among you seems to be wise in this age, let him become a fool that he may become wise. For the wisdom of this world is foolishness with God" (1 Corinthians 3:18–19).

Jesus said,
"I am the way,
the truth, and
the life.
No one comes to the Father
except through Me."

—John 14:6

"Do not marvel, my brethren, if the world hates you."

—1 JOHN 3:13

Why do evangelicals try so desperately to court the world's favor? Churches plan their worship services to cater to the "unchurched." Christian performers ape every worldly fad in music and entertainment. Preachers are terrified that the offense of the gospel might turn someone against them; so they deliberately omit the parts of the message the world might not like.

Evangelicalism seems to have been hijacked by legions of carnal spin-doctors, who are trying their best to convince the world that the church can be just as inclusive, pluralistic, and broad-minded as the most politically-correct worldling.

The quest for the world's approval is nothing less than spiritual harlotry. In fact, that is precisely the imagery the apostle James used to describe it. He wrote, "Adulterers and adulteresses! Do you not know that friendship with the world is enmity with God? Whoever therefore wants to be a friend of the world makes himself an enemy of God" (James 4:4).

There is and always has been a fundamental, irreconcilable incompatibility between the church and the world. Christian thought is out of harmony with all the world's philosophies. Genuine faith in Christ entails a denial of every worldly value. Biblical truth contradicts all the world's religions. Christianity itself is therefore antithetical to virtually everything this world admires.

Jesus told His disciples, "If the world hates you, you know that it hated Me before it hated you. If you were of the world, the world would love its own. Yet because you are not of the world, but I chose you out of the world, therefore the world hates you" (John 15:18–19).

Notice that our Lord considered it a given that the

world would despise the church. Far from teaching His disciples to try to win the world's favor by reinventing the gospel to suit worldly preferences, Jesus expressly warned that the quest for worldly accolades is a characteristic of false prophets: "Woe to you when all men speak well of you, for so did their fathers to the false prophets" (Luke 6:26).

He further explained, "The world . . . hates Me because I testify of it that its works are evil" (John 7:7). In other words, the world's contempt for Christianity stems from moral, not intellectual, motives: "And this is the condemnation, that the light has come into the world, and men loved darkness rather than light, because their deeds were evil. For everyone practicing evil hates the light and does not come to the light, lest his deeds should be exposed" (John 3:19–20). That is why no matter how dramatically worldly opinion might vary, Christian truth will never be popular with the world.

Yet, in virtually every era of church history, there have been people in the church who are convinced that the best way to win the world is by catering to worldly tastes. Such an approach has always been to the detriment of the gospel message. The only times the church has made any significant impact on the world are when the people of God have stood firm, refused to compromise, and boldly proclaimed the truth despite the world's hostility. When Christians have shrunk away from the task of confronting popular worldly delusions with unpopular biblical truths, the church has invariably lost influence and impotently blended into the world. Both Scripture and history attest to that fact.

And the Christian message simply *cannot* be twisted to conform to the vicissitudes of worldly opinion. Biblical truth is fixed and constant, not subject to change or adaptation. Worldly opinion, on the other hand, is in constant flux. The various fads and philosophies that dominate the world change radically and regularly from generation to generation. The only thing that remains constant is the world's hatred of Christ and His gospel.

In all likelihood, the world will not long embrace whatever ideology is in vogue this year. If the pattern of history is any indicator, by the time our great grandchildren become adults, worldly opinion will be dominated by a completely new system of belief and a whole different set of values. Tomorrow's generation will renounce all of today's fads and philosophies. But one thing will remain unchanged: Until the Lord Himself returns and establishes His kingdom on earth, whatever ideology gains popularity in the world will be as hostile to biblical truth as all its predecessors have been.

MODERNISM

Consider the record of the past century, for example. A hundred years ago, the church was beset by *modernism*. Modernism was a worldview based on the notion that only science could explain reality. The modernist, in effect, began with the presupposition that nothing supernatural is real.

It ought to have been instantly obvious that modernism and Christianity were incompatible at the most fundamental level. If nothing supernatural is real, then much of the Bible is untrue and has no authority; the incarnation of Christ is a myth (nullifying Christ's authority as well); and all the supernatural elements of Christianity, including God Himself, must be utterly redefined in naturalistic terms. Modernism was anti-Christian at its core.

Nonetheless, the visible church at the beginning of the twentieth century was filled with people who were convinced modernism and Christianity could and should be reconciled. They insisted that if the church did not keep in step with the times by embracing modernism, Christianity would not survive the twentieth century. The church would become increasingly irrelevant to modern people, they said, and soon it would die. So they devised a "social gospel" devoid of the true gospel of salvation.

Of course, *biblical* Christianity survived the twentieth

century just fine. Wherever Christians remained committed to the truthfulness and authority of Scripture, the church flourished. But ironically, those churches and denominations that embraced modernism were the ones that became increasingly irrelevant and all but died out before the century was over. Many grandiose but nearly empty stone buildings offer mute testimony to the deadliness of compromise with modernism.

POSTMODERNISM

Modernism is now regarded as yesterday's way of thinking. The dominant worldview in secular and academic circles today is called *postmodernism*.

Postmodernists have repudiated modernism's absolute confidence in science as the only pathway to the truth. In fact, postmodernism has completely lost interest in "the truth," insisting that there is no such thing as absolute, objective, or universal truth.

Modernism was indeed folly and needed to be

abandoned. But postmodernism is a tragic step in the wrong direction. Unlike modernism, which was still concerned with whether basic convictions, beliefs, and ideologies are objectively true or false, postmodernism simply denies that any truth can be objectively known.

To the postmodernist, reality is whatever the individual imagines it to be. That means what is "true" is determined subjectively by each person, and there is no such thing as objective, authoritative truth that governs or applies to all humanity universally. The postmodernist naturally believes it is pointless to argue whether opinion A is superior to opinion B. After all, if reality is merely a construct of the human mind, one person's perspective of truth is ultimately just as good as another's.

Having given up on knowing objective truth, the postmodernist occupies himself instead with the quest for "understanding" the other person's point of view. So the words *truth* and *understanding* take on radical new meanings. Ironically, "understanding" requires that we first of all disavow the possibility of knowing any truth at all. And "truth" becomes nothing more than a personal opinion, usually best kept to oneself.

That is the one essential, non-negotiable demand postmodernism makes of everyone: We are not supposed to think we know any objective truth. Postmodernists often suggest that every opinion should be shown equal respect. And therefore on the surface, postmodernism seems driven by a broad-minded concern for harmony and tolerance. It all sounds very charitable and altruistic. But what really underlies the postmodernist belief system is an utter *intolerance* for every worldview that makes any universal truth-claims—particularly biblical Christianity.

In other words, postmodernism begins with a presupposition that is irreconcilable with the objective, divinely-revealed truth of Scripture. Like modernism, postmodernism is fundamentally and diametrically opposed to the gospel of Jesus Christ.

POSTMODERNISM AND THE CHURCH

Nonetheless, the church today is filled with people who are advocating postmodern ideas. Some of them do it self-consciously and deliberately, but most do it unwittingly. (Having imbibed too much of the spirit of the age, they are simply regurgitating worldly opinion.) The evangelical movement as a whole, still recovering from its long battle with modernism, is not prepared for a new and different adversary. Many Christians have therefore not yet recognized the extreme danger posed by postmodernist thought.

Postmodernism's influence has clearly infected the church already. Evangelicals are toning down their message so that the gospel's stark truth-claims don't sound so jarring to the postmodern ear. Many shy away from stating unequivocally that the Bible is true and all other religious systems and worldviews are false. Some who call themselves Christians have gone even further, purposefully denying the exclusivity of

Christ and openly questioning His claim that He is the only way to God.

The biblical message is clear. Jesus said, "I am the way, the truth, and the life. No one comes to the Father except through Me" (John 14:6). The apostle Peter proclaimed to a hostile audience, "Nor is there salvation in any other, for there is no other name under heaven given among men by which we must be saved" (Acts 4:12). The apostle John wrote, "He who does not believe the Son shall not see life, but the wrath of God abides on him" (John 3:36). Again and again, Scripture stresses that Jesus Christ is the only hope of salvation for the world. "For there is one God and one Mediator between God and men, the Man Christ Jesus" (1 Timothy 2:5). Only Christ can atone for sin, and therefore only Christ can provide salvation. "And this is the testimony: that God has given us eternal life, and this life is in His Son. He who has the Son has life; he who does not have the Son of God does not have life" (1 John 5:11–12).

Those truths are antithetical to the central tenet of

postmodernism. They make exclusive, universal truth-claims declaring Christ the only true way to heaven and all other belief-systems erroneous. That is what Scripture teaches. It is what the true church has proclaimed throughout her history. It is the message of Christianity. And it simply cannot be adjusted to accommodate postmodern sensitivities.

Instead, many Christians just pass over the exclusive claims of Christ in embarrassed silence. Even worse, some in the church, including a few of evangelicalism's best-known leaders, have begun to suggest that perhaps people *can* be saved apart from knowing Christ.

Christians cannot capitulate to postmodernism without sacrificing the very essence of our faith. The Bible's claim that Christ is the only way of salvation is certainly out of harmony with the postmodern notion of "tolerance." But it is, after all, just what the Bible plainly teaches. And the Bible, not postmodern opinion, is the supreme authority for the Christian. The Bible alone should determine what we believe and proclaim to the world. We cannot waver on this, no matter how much this postmodern world complains that our beliefs make us "intolerant."

TOLERANT INTOLERANCE

Postmodernism's veneration of tolerance is its most obvious feature. But the version of "tolerance" peddled by postmodernists is actually a twisted and dangerous corruption of true virtue.

Incidentally, tolerance is never mentioned in the Bible as a virtue, except in the sense of patience, forbearance, and longsuffering (cf. Ephesians 4:2.) In fact, the contemporary notion of tolerance is a pathetically feeble concept compared to the love Scripture commands Christians to show even to their enemies. Jesus said, "Love your enemies, do good to those who hate you, bless those who curse you, and pray for those who spitefully use you" (Luke 6:27–28; cf. vv. 29–36).

When our grandparents spoke of tolerance as a

virtue, they had something like that in mind. The word once meant respecting people and treating them kindly even when we believe they are wrong. But the postmodern notion of tolerance means we must never regard anyone else's opinions as wrong. Biblical tolerance is for people; postmodern tolerance is for ideas.

Accepting every belief as equally valid is hardly a real virtue, but it is practically the only kind of virtue postmodernism knows anything about. Traditional virtues (including humility, self-control, and chastity) are openly scorned, and even regarded as transgressions, in the world of postmodernism.

Predictably, the beatification of postmodern tolerance has had a disastrous effect on real virtue in our society. In this age of tolerance, what was once forbidden is now encouraged. What was once universally deemed immoral is now celebrated. Marital infidelity and divorce have been normalized. Profanity is commonplace. Abortion, homosexuality, and moral perversions of all kinds are championed by large advocacy groups and enthusiastically promoted by the popular media. The postmodern notion of tolerance is systematically turning genuine virtue on its head.

Just about the only remaining taboo is the naïve and politically incorrect notion that another person's alternative lifestyle, religion, or different perspective is wrong.

One major exception to that rule stands out starkly: It is OK for postmodernists to be intolerant of those who claim they know the truth, particularly biblical Christians. In fact, those who fancy themselves the leading advocates of tolerance today are often the most outspoken opponents of evangelical Christianity.

Look on the World Wide Web, for example, and see what is being said by the self-styled champions of religious tolerance. What you'll find is a great deal of *intolerance* for Bible-based Christianity. In fact, some of the most bitterly anti-Christian material on the World Wide Web can be found at sites supposedly promoting religious tolerance.[1]

Why is that? Why does authentic biblical Christianity find such ferocious opposition from people who think they are paragons of tolerance? It is because the truth-claims of Scripture—and particularly Jesus' claim to be the *only* way to God—are diametrically opposed to the fundamental presuppositions of the postmodern mind. The Christian message represents a death blow to the postmodernist worldview.

But as long as Christians are being duped or intimidated into softening the bold claims of Christ and widening the narrow road, the church will make no headway against postmodernism. We need to recover the distinctiveness of the gospel. We need to regain our confidence in the power of God's truth. And we need to proclaim boldly that Christ is the *only* true hope for the people of this world.

That may not be what people want to hear in this pseudo-tolerant age of postmodernism. But it is true nonetheless. And precisely *because* it is true and the gospel of Christ is the only hope for a lost world, it is all the more urgent that we rise above all the voices of confusion in the world and say so.

The remainder of this book will examine six key concepts that explain the distinctiveness of Christianity. These are principles that flatly contradict the conventional wisdom of postmodernism. But they are essential components of a biblical worldview. These six principles, defined by six key words, build upon one another and interconnect in such a way that they stand or fall together. They give us the necessary framework for thinking, for making sense of the world around us, and for ministering in this postmodern age.

"Thy word is truth."

—JOHN 17:17

*A*uthentic Christianity starts with the premise that there is a source of truth outside of us. Specifically, God's Word is truth (Psalm 119:151; John 17:17). It is *objectively* true—meaning it is true whether it speaks subjectively to any given individual or not; it is true regardless of how anyone feels about it; it is true for everyone universally and without exception; it is *absolutely* true.

That, of course, contradicts the basic presupposition that governs most people's thinking today. Postmodern philosophy says there is no such thing as absolute truth or if there is, it is unknowable. According to pos modernism, truth is nothing more than a creation of t

human mind; people determine their own reality; and therefore no one has *the* truth.

Above all, the postmodernist is convinced that no religion is superior to any other. We are not supposed to think our beliefs are necessarily valid for anyone else. Nor should *any* theological position ever be thought of as right or wrong. What I believe is valid for me; and whatever you believe is equally valid for you. And thus we can affirm each other's religions, even if our beliefs flatly contradict one another. That is the postmodernist credo.

You may not realize how deeply this sort of thinking has penetrated the modern consciousness, but it has already taken over the academic and secular world. Two months after the September 11, 2001, terrorist attacks on the World Trade Center and the Pentagon, former U.S. President Bill Clinton gave a speech at Georgetown University in which he suggested that America's own "arrogant self-righteousness" was partly to blame for making the nation a target of terrorism. Apparently

Clinton believed the whole mess could have been avoided if everyone on both sides had simply realized there is no such thing as absolute or universal truth, and therefore no ideology is worth fighting over.

"Nobody's got the truth," he told students. "You're at a university which basically believes that no one ever has the whole truth, ever. . . . We are incapable of ever having the whole truth." The terrorists, Clinton suggested, are being brutal and intolerant only because they believe they have the truth, whereas our society's more tolerant attitudes are rooted in an understanding that absolute truth is unknowable: "They believe they got it. Because we don't believe you can have the whole truth, we think everybody counts."[1]

Those remarks pretty much sum up secular society's current attitude. Skepticism has been enthroned and consecrated, while confident faith has been banished and demonized. The only thing we can be certain about is that we can't be certain of anything. To hold strong convictions about anything (other than our own inability to discover truth) is deemed inherently intolerant, even evil. Furthermore, according to the postmodernist way of thinking, there is little point in trying to combat false ideas with true ones. After all, they say, if we claim *we* have the truth, we become just as evil as the terrorists. So instead, the postmodernist intelligentsia are doing their best to disabuse everyone of the archaic notion that absolute, objective truth is knowable at all.

That view is shaping the world in which we live. People have abandoned the quest for objective truth. Multitudes literally and wholeheartedly believe they can make their own reality and define their own truth. The popularity of such a philosophy accounts for the rise of New Age religion and ideology. It also explains why people today are more self-absorbed and narcissistic than practically any generation in history.

Former President Clinton was suggesting it is arrogant to think anyone can know absolute truth. But the real arrogance is that of the person who thinks he can invent his own truth on the fly. When everything "depends on what your definition of *is* is"—when individuals can reimagine and reinterpret *everything* subjectively so that each person determines what is right in his own eyes—civilization itself is in serious trouble.

That is the direction our society is headed. Having accepted the notion that absolute truth is unknowable, people are willing to accept almost anything in place of the truth.

Even in the church, there has been a serious erosion of confidence in the objective truth of Scripture. Dogmatism on any point of doctrine is generally out of vogue; uncertainty and openness to multiple points of view is the preferred style among preachers and teachers these days. The most popular mass movements in evangeli-calism today are ecumenical in their thrust, urging us to set aside doctrine for the sake of harmony. Such trends reflect a capitulation to the postmodern idea that absolute truth is unknowable and therefore it doesn't really matter much anyway.

Postmodernism's contempt for objective truth is

slipping into the church in more subtle ways, too. Attend the typical evangelical home Bible study meeting and you will probably be invited to share your opinion about "what this verse means to *me*," as if the message of Scripture were unique to every individual. Rare is the teacher who is concerned with what Scripture means to *God*.

But if we really believe Scripture is the Word of God, why should we balk at saying it has an objective meaning; it is absolutely true; and all other interpretations are false? Evangelicals have always believed that Scripture is *perspicuous*—its essential meaning is evident on its face. It is not a secret or a mystery to be solved. The Bible is God's revelation to us. It is a disclosure of the truth; it is not a puzzle. And in all essential matters, it speaks with perfect clarity.

Certainly there are in Scripture "some things hard to understand, which untaught and unstable people twist to their own destruction" (2 Peter 3:16). There are also many matters of secondary importance over which we do not need to contend fiercely. On such indifferent matters, the rule is clear: "Let each be fully convinced in his own mind" (Romans 14:5). But the main gist of Scripture, and the gospel message in particular, is clear and unambiguous. It was not given by "private interpretation," and its meaning is not subject to individual preferences. "For prophecy never came by the will of man, but holy men of God spoke as they were moved by the Holy Spirit" (2 Peter 1:20–21).

Again and again, Scripture makes these claims for itself: "All Scripture is given by inspiration of God, and is profitable for doctrine, for reproof, for correction, for instruction in righteousness, that the man of God may be complete, thoroughly equipped for every good work" (2 Timothy 3:16–17). In other words, Scripture is not only inspired by God, but it is also sufficient to equip us thoroughly with all the spiritual truth we need. It is "more sure" than our own senses (2 Peter 1:19, KJV). It endures forever (1 Peter 1:25). It is trustworthy in every jot and tittle (Matthew 5:18). It is unchanging and eternal

(Isaiah 40:8). Jesus Himself said, "Heaven and earth will pass away, but My words will by no means pass away" (Matthew 24:35).

Authentic Christianity has always held that Scripture is absolute, objective truth. It is as true for one person as it is for another, regardless of anyone's opinion about it. It has one true meaning that applies to everyone. It is God's Word to humanity, and its true meaning is determined by God; it is not something that can be shaped to fit the preferences of individual hearers.

Scripture is absolutely true whether it affects you and me or not. Scripture would be true whether we ever lived or not. In no way is the truth of Scripture decided by anyone's experience. Whether it affects us or doesn't affect us subjectively has nothing to do with its actual meaning or its truthfulness. The message of Scripture is not malleable. It is not unique to each person. It is not determined by personal experience or personal opinion.

That deals a heavy blow to a very large segment of professing Christianity today. Multitudes are listening for the voice of God in their heads or seeking some kind of intuitive epiphany in which truth is revealed to them subjectively. But the only ultimate and absolute truth for the Christian—the truth that supersedes all private opinions, personal feelings, and subjective experiences—is the objective truth of God as revealed in the Scriptures when rightly interpreted.

Biblical truth is objective. It is true by itself. It is true whether or not we feel it's true. It is true whether or not it has been validated by someone's experience. It is true because *God* says it is true. It is wholly true, and it is true down to the smallest jot and tittle. Psalm 119:160 says, "The entirety of Your word is truth, and every one of Your righteous judgments endures forever."

That is the very starting point and the necessary foundation for a truly Christian worldview. Give up the ground of biblical truth, and whatever belief system you have left is not worthy to be labeled Christian, even if it retains vestiges of Christian symbolism and terminology.

Many who would call themselves Christians today are

in precisely that situation. They use the language and symbolism of Christianity, but their real source of authority is something besides Scripture. Some simply live by their feelings and shape their beliefs in accord with their own personal preferences. Others actually claim God speaks directly to them through voices, strong impressions, or vague feelings which they interpret as direct revelations from the Holy Spirit. Still others think of the Scriptures as an improvisational script, which they can modify or interpret any way they please. In any case, their lives and beliefs are ordered in accord with their own personal preferences. Their beliefs are really no different from those of the New Agers who believe truth is found within themselves.

But historic Christianity is based on the objective revelation of Scripture. That is why our first key word for describing the Christian worldview is *objectivity*. Our faith is grounded in the conviction that God has spoken, and His Word is objective truth. What He has given us is absolute and unshakable. It is the truth by which all other truth-claims are measured.

"I have not written to you because you do not know the truth,
but because you know it, and that no lie is of the truth."

—1 John 2:21

A second key word that helps define an authentically Christian worldview is *rationality*. We believe the objective revelation of Scripture is rational. The Bible makes good sense. It contains no contradictions, no errors, and no unsound principles. Anything that *does* contradict Scripture is untrue.

That sort of rationality is antithetical to the whole gist of postmodern thought. People today are taught to glorify contradiction, to embrace that which is absurd, to prefer that which is subjective, and to let feelings (rather than intellect) determine what they believe. They are taught not to reject ideas just because they contradict what we believe to be true. And they are even encouraged to embrace contradictory concepts and afford them all the same respect *as if* they were true. Such irrationality is nothing less than an overt rejection of the very concept of truth.

As Christians we know that God cannot lie (Titus 1:2). He cannot deny Himself (2 Timothy 2:13); and therefore He does not contradict Himself. He is not the author of confusion (1 Corinthians 14:33). His truth is perfectly self-consistent.

That means, first of all, that the Word of God is a precise and unassailable record of truth. The Bible is not filled with absurdities, contradictions, or fantasies. It is perfectly consistent with itself and perfectly consistent with all that is true. The facts set forth in Scripture are reliable. The historical events described in the Bible are true history, not a mythical or fanciful allegory. The doctrine taught there is without error. The details of Scripture are accurate details, from day one of creation to the ultimate consummation of Christ's return. Scripture itself is completely free of all errors and deficiencies. "It is easier for heaven and earth to pass away than for one tittle of the law to fail" (Luke 16:17). That is how Christ viewed Scripture, and anyone who takes a different approach is not in that respect a genuine follower of Christ.

But there's a second, equally important, implication of our confidence in God's absolute truthfulness: Since His Word is objectively true and perfectly reliable in everything it teaches, Scripture should be both the starting point and the final test of truth in all our thinking. If Scripture is wholly true, then anything that contradicts Scripture is simply false, even if we're talking about the fundamental beliefs upon which the world's most popular ideologies are based.

That sort of black-and-white rationality is one of the main reasons biblical Christianity is intolerable in a generation that despises the very idea of absolute truth.

Lest anyone misunderstand, we are not advocating *rationalism*—the notion that human reason alone, apart from any supernatural revelation, can discover truth. A rationalist imagines that human reason is both the source and the final test of all truth. In effect, rationalists exalt human reason above Scripture.

As Christians we oppose *rationalism*, but Christianity is by no means hostile to *rationality*. We believe the truth is logical; it is coherent; it is intelligible. Not only can truth be known rationally; it cannot be known at all if we abandon rationality.

Irrationality is an assault on the Scripture and the intent of God. When God gave the Bible, He meant for it to be *understood*. But it can be understood only by those who apply their minds to it rationally. Contrary to what many assume, the meaning of Scripture is not something that comes to us through mystical means. It is not spiritual secret that must be uncovered by some arcane or arbitrary method. Its true meaning may be understood *only* by those who approach it rationally and sensibly.

Nehemiah 8 describes the revival that took place in the time of Nehemiah. It was sparked by the public reading of the Scriptures. Nehemiah describes the scene:

Now all the people gathered together as one man in the open square that was in front of the Water Gate; and they told Ezra the scribe to bring the Book of the Law of Moses, which the LORD had commanded Israel. So Ezra the priest brought the Law before the assembly of men and women and all who could hear with understanding on the first day of the seventh month. Then he read from it in the open square that was in front of the Water Gate from morning until midday, before the men and women and those who could understand; and the ears of all the people were attentive to the Book of the Law. (Nehemiah 8:1–3)

Notice the stress on the people's attentiveness. The reading was for the benefit of those "who could hear with understanding . . . those who could understand." Verse 8 describes how Ezra and the scribes did the reading: "They read distinctly from the book, in the Law of God; and they gave the sense, and helped them to understand the reading."

The reading wasn't a ritual exercise, like a chant or the ceremonial intoning of some liturgy. It was aimed at the people's cognitive faculties—their rational minds.

The power of the Word of God lies in its *meaning*, not merely in the sound of the words. It is not a magical incantation, where its power might be unleashed through merely reciting syllables. But the power inherent in Scripture is the power of truth. I like to say that the *meaning* of the Scripture *is* the Scripture. If you don't have the interpretation of the passage right, then you don't have the Word of God, because only the true meaning *is* the Word of God.

It's not as if we can make the words mean anything we want them to mean, so that whatever connotation we impose on the words *becomes* the Word of God. Only the true interpretation of the text is the authentic Word of God, and any other interpretation is simply not what God is saying. Remember, God's Word is objective truth revealed, and therefore it has a rational meaning. That meaning, and that meaning alone, is the truth. Getting it right is of supreme importance.

That is why it is so critical that we interpret Scripture carefully in order to understand it correctly. It is a rational process, not a mystical or whimsical one.

Is it a *spiritual* process? Absolutely. I never approach my study of the Word of God without praying, "Lord, open my understanding to see the truth." But I don't then sit there until something falls out of the sky; I open my books and pursue a rational understanding of the text.

It starts with the understanding that Scripture is internally self-consistent. Therefore, as we compare Scripture with Scripture, the clear parts explain the more difficult parts. The more we study, the more light is shed on our understanding. It is hard mental work, but it is *spiritual* work nonetheless.

In fact, we are utterly dependent on the Holy Spirit to teach us truth, because "The natural man does not receive the things of the Spirit of God, for they are foolishness to him; nor can he know them, because they are spiritually discerned" (1 Corinthians 2:14). But the way the Holy Spirit gives us understanding is through our minds—employing our rational faculties (v. 16; Ephesians 1:18; 4:23; 2 Timothy 1:7).

Neo-orthodox theology, which rose to prominence in the first half of the twentieth century, has caused a tremendous amount of confusion about the rationality of truth. Neo-orthodox theologians insist that Christianity is an irrational belief system—a religion of "paradox." What they really are suggesting is that Christianity is full of contradictions. *Paradox* is a misnomer in the sense that they use it. A true paradox is a play on words, such as "Many who are first will be last, and the last first" (Matthew 19:30), and "Whoever desires to become great among you, let him be your servant" (Matthew 20:26). But when the neo-orthodox use the term *paradox*, they are speaking of a real contradiction. They regard all truth as irrational, self-contradictory, and absurd to the logical mind. Faith in their system entails the abandonment of logic. It is a blind leap into the abyss of irrationalism. They borrowed their irrationalism from existential philosophy and made it the hallmark of their theology. In doing so, they laid the groundwork for a postmodern version of Christianity.[1] But it is not *true* Christianity, because it has abandoned the rationality that is essential to truth itself.

The problem with such irrationalism is that it nullifies the law of non-contradiction, the essential ground of all rational thinking. If two contradictory propositions can both be true simultaneously, then an idea that opposes the truth cannot necessarily be deemed error. The antithesis of a true statement cannot automatically be judged false. That is the very same kind of thinking that lies at the heart of postmodernist tolerance. It is not a Christian view of truth. It is irrationalism.

The apostle Paul wrote, "If anyone advocates a different doctrine and does not agree with sound words, those of our Lord Jesus Christ, and with the doctrine conforming to godliness, he is conceited and understands nothing" (1 Timothy 6:3–4, NASB). Paul's statement assumes that the truth is rational and whatever contradicts the truth is error. That is the proper Christian understanding of biblical truth. It is the antithesis of postmodern thinking.

There *are* some difficult tensions in Christian doctrine. For example, we believe God is sovereign over the human will ("The king's heart is in the hand of the LORD, like the rivers of water; He turns it wherever He wishes." Proverbs 21:1). And yet we believe people choose freely in accord with their desires so that each one of us is morally responsible for our actions ("Each of us shall give account of himself to God." Romans 14:12). Many find those truths difficult to reconcile; and yet there is no actual contradiction between them. God's sovereignty is not at odds with human responsibility. The two principles work in perfect harmony, even though it is not immediately obvious to us *how* they work. We also believe in the Trinity—that God is one in essence and yet He exists in three Persons. Some have tried to characterize that doctrine as self-contradictory, but it is not. We don't believe God is three in the same sense He is one. Such truths are not contradictions; they are not even paradoxes in the sense neo-orthodoxy uses the term. They are difficult truths that, if anything, require us to exercise extra care in applying logical rigor. But we are not to think of them as irrational. They are not.

Irrationality is tantamount to a denial of all truth. Precisely because we believe the Bible is objectively true, we insist it *must* be understood and interpreted rationally.

Chapter Four: Veracity

"And now, O Lord GOD, You are God, and Your words are true."
—2 SAMUEL 7:28

A third word that establishes the framework for a Christian worldview is *veracity*. Authentic Christianity, as we have been seeing, is concerned first and foremost with *truth*. The Christian faith is not primarily about feelings, although deep feelings will surely result from the impact of truth on our hearts. It is not about human relationships, even though relationships are the main focus in many of today's evangelical pulpits. It is not about success and earthly blessings, no matter how much one might get that impression from watching the programs that dominate religious television these days.

Biblical Christianity is all about *truth*. God's objective revelation (the Bible) interpreted rationally yields divine truth in perfectly sufficient measure. Everything we need to know for life and godliness is there for us in Scripture (2 Peter 1:3). God wrote only one book—the Bible. It contains all the truth by which He intended us to order our spiritual lives. We don't need to consult any other source for spiritual or moral principles. Scripture is not only wholly truth; it is also the highest standard of all truth—the rule by which all truth-claims must be measured.

Such a conviction is the very antithesis of the postmodern notion that no one should ever claim to know objective truth. And that is another major reason why Christianity has been targeted by the proponents of postmodern inclusivism.

Authentic Christianity is "the faith which was once for all delivered to the saints" (Jude 3). Christian truth is not subject to change or amendment. It isn't nullified by changes in worldly opinion or standards of political correctness. It doesn't need to be adapted and redefined for every new generation.

Certainly, an individual's understanding of the truth can be refined and sharpened by study of the Scripture. But the truth itself does not need to be reinvented or retooled in order to make it suitable for the times in which we live. The same truth Abraham, Moses, David, and the apostles believed is still truth for us. Changing times do not change the truth. Scripture is as unchanging as God Himself: "But the word of the LORD endures forever" (1 Peter 1:25). In other words, we need to adapt our understanding to the truth of God's Word, not try to manipulate Scripture in a vain effort to harmonize it with the changing opinions of this world.

The truth of Scripture is something precious that must be carefully handled and closely guarded (1 Timothy 6:20). Once again, a proper understanding of Scripture involves conscientious and diligent study. Second Timothy 2:15 says, "Be diligent to present yourself approved to God, a worker who does not need to be ashamed, rightly dividing the word of truth." By implication we see that all who do not divide the Scriptures right are sloppy workers who *ought* to be ashamed. The phrase "rightly dividing" comes from a Greek expression that means "cutting it straight."

Paul was drawing on his experience as a tentmaker and applying a principle learned from that craft to Bible interpretation. Tents were made of material like goat hides. Since goats are relatively small animals, no one skin would ever be big enough to make a tent. Therefore the tentmaker would cut several goat hides according to a pattern and sew them together to make one large tent. Obviously, if the pieces weren't cut straight, they wouldn't fit together right. So when the Apostle Paul says we are to cut the Scripture straight, he means that individual passages of Scripture are to be interpreted so that the whole fits perfectly together in a coherent, self-consistent way.

In other words, no one has the right to be a theologian who is not an exegete. You can't make sense of the whole until you fit the pieces together properly. And if you're butchering the pieces, they won't fit together right.

Misinterpretations won't ultimately fit together into a coherent whole. You have to interpret the individual passages correctly (cut them straight). You do that by comparing Scripture with Scripture—again, letting Scripture itself be the rule by which we interpret Scripture. When that is done correctly—when you've rightly understood the texts of Scripture—then they fit together, and the whole comes together in the way God designed.

Precisely because it is "the word of *truth*," both in the whole and in the parts, Scripture fits together perfectly. That perfect fit is one of the ways we know we have interpreted individual sections of Scripture correctly. So Scripture, rightly interpreted, yields truth. And that truth is to be the substance of our message.

In Paul's day, like today, there were men who sought positions of prominence in ministry and church leadership but were not really concerned for the truth. They made up their own message as they went. They were apparently looking for prestige or influence, or some other more sinister kind of fleshly self-gratification.

Their teaching therefore twisted the truth. Paul referred to it as "profane and idle babblings" (2 Timothy 2:16). That statement follows immediately after his charge to Timothy about "rightly dividing the word of truth."

He writes, "But shun profane and idle babblings, for they will increase to more ungodliness. And their message will spread like cancer. Hymenaeus and Philetus are of this sort, who have strayed concerning the truth, saying that the resurrection is already past; and they overthrow the faith of some" (vv. 16–18).

Notice that the apostle Paul didn't mind naming names. He wasn't concerned with political correctness; he was concerned with the *truth*. And the purveyors of lies needed to be identified and answered with the truth. Their twisting of the truth was actually overthrowing the faith of some.

Truth and faith are inextricably linked together. People cannot have genuine faith apart from the truth. Real faith involves the assent of the mind and the submission of the will to the truth. So if you remove truth from the equation, you overthrow faith, as Hymenaeus and Philetus were doing.

Did you realize that the truth is instrumental in salvation? People cannot be saved apart from hearing and embracing the *truth*. Romans 6:17 says, "Though you were slaves of sin, yet you obeyed from the heart that form of doctrine to which you were delivered." In other words, people are saved when they are delivered out of error into sound doctrine—*truth*. There is a real sense in which we are saved by the truth. Peter writes, "You have purified your souls in obeying the truth" (1 Peter 1:22). We are begotten by the word of truth (v. 23).

So the truth is everything to a Christian. That is why we are called to refute error, defend the truth, and proclaim Scripture as the supreme truth against every lie propagated by the world.

I fear that the church in this postmodern era has lost focus on that fact. It is no longer deemed necessary to fight for the truth. In fact, many evangelicals now consider it ill-mannered and uncharitable to argue about *any* point of doctrine. Even gross error is now tolerable in some quarters for the sake of peace. Rather than rightly dividing the Word and proclaiming it as truth, many churches now feature motivational lectures, drama, comedy, and other forms of entertainment—while ignoring the great doctrines of the faith. Meanwhile, people who attack the truth in pseudo-scholarly ways are finding publishers in the evangelical realm and being honored as if they had deep insight.

We must recover our love for biblical truth, as well as our conviction that it is unassailable truth. *We have the truth* in a world where most people are simply wandering around in hopeless ignorance. We need to proclaim it from the housetops and quit playing along with those who suggest we are being arrogant if we claim to know anything for certain. We *do* have the truth, not because we are smarter or better than anyone else, but because God has revealed it in the Scriptures and has been gracious to open our eyes to see it. We would be sinning if we tried to keep the truth to ourselves.

"They were astonished at His teaching, for He taught them as one having authority, and not as the scribes."

—MARK 1:22

*A*n understanding of the Bible's *authority* is the fourth foundation stone for a proper Christian worldview. Because we believe Scripture is true, we must proclaim it with conviction and without compromise or apology. The Bible makes bold claims, and Christians who believe it ought to affirm it boldly.

Anyone who faithfully and correctly proclaims the Word of God *will* speak with authority. It is not our own authority. It is not even the ecclesiastical authority attached to the office of a pastor or teacher in the church. It is a still greater authority than that. Insofar as our teaching accurately reflects the truth of Scripture, it has the full weight of *God's own authority* behind it.

49

That is a staggering thought, but it is precisely how 1 Peter 4:11 instructs us to handle biblical truth: "If anyone speaks, let him speak as the oracles of God."

Of course that is a profound threat to the tolerance of a society that loves its sin and thinks of compromise as a good thing. To speak boldly and declare that God has spoken with finality is neither stylish nor politically correct. But if we truly believe the Bible is the Word of God, how can we handle it any other way?

Many modern evangelicals, cowed by post-modernism's demand for latitudinarianism, claim they believe Scripture, but then shy away from proclaiming it with any authority. They are willing to give lip service to the truth of Scripture, but in practice they strip it of its authority, treating it as just another opinion in the great mix of postmodern ideas.

Neither Scripture nor common sense will allow for such a view. If the Bible is true, then it is also authoritative. As divinely revealed truth, it carries the full weight of God's own authority. If you claim to believe the Bible at all, you ultimately must bow to its authority. That means making it the final arbiter of truth—the rule by which every other opinion is evaluated.

The Bible is not just another idea to be thrown into the public discussion and accepted or rejected as the individual sees fit. It is the Word of God, and it demands to be received as such, to the exclusion of all other opinions.

Obviously *that* way of assessing truth is unpopular today. According to the new postmodern tolerance, everyone is entitled to have whatever opinion he or she prefers; every belief is to be accorded equal respect; and no one is ever supposed to claim superiority for any single viewpoint. In effect, then, postmodern tolerance entails an utter rejection of the whole concept of divine authority. It amounts to a denial that God has truly spoken, or at the very least, a denial that His words have any real authority. That is precisely why postmodern tolerance is fundamentally at odds with a biblical worldview.

As Christians, we face a clear choice: Either go

along with the spirit of the age and downplay the authority of Scripture, or accept Scripture and set its authority and ourselves against the rest of the world. Our duty is clear (James 4:4).

And yet it seems that many of the most vocal and visible leaders in the evangelical community are fearful of asserting biblical authority. Rarely do evangelical spokesmen speak clearly to the world with an authoritative "Thus saith the Lord." How have we reached the point where we can accept as authoritative the opinion of a lawyer, a doctor, or an architect, but we will not tolerate an authoritative word from God?

Do evangelicals still believe without reservation that biblical truth has divine authority? Evidently not. It has become trendy to speak of the clash between truth and error as a "dialogue." Every time a conflict arises between Christianity and another worldview, some evangelical leader will issue a call for dialogue with leading advocates of the other point of view. Over the past decade or so, well known evangelical leaders have sponsored formal dialogues with a wide variety of non-Christian religious figures, cult leaders, advocates of various alternative lifestyles, and representatives of practically every worldview that is hostile to biblical Christianity.

Shortly after the September 11 terrorist event, one of the best known evangelical churches in America sponsored a dialogue with an Islamic cleric *(imam)* in their weekend worship services, ostensibly to bring Christians and Muslims closer together. "I thought it was interesting how much we have in common," one church member told a reporter after the meeting. Another said the dialogue with the *imam* had "opened up doors to communicate and showed [Muslims are] people just like we are." According to a reporter who covered the event, those responses were "the kind of impact [the pastor] had hoped for."[1]

Why is it that the goal of such dialogue *always* seems to be to minimize the differences between Christianity and false religion—and never to draw the lines of distinction more clearly?

Biblical truth is to be proclaimed with authority, not put on the table for discussion as just one possible alternative to other points of view. The conflict between biblical truth and competing beliefs is not a matter to be settled by dialogue. This is spiritual warfare, not a tea party. It should be seen as combat, not a conversation. We are commanded to pull down the strongholds of unbiblical thinking, "casting down arguments and every high thing that exalts itself against the knowledge of God, bringing every thought into captivity to the obedience of Christ" (2 Corinthians 10:5).

But the church has become so effeminate and powerless these days that most evangelicals seem to think such a militant stance against error is inappropriate and too severe. Christians have virtually surrendered the battle for truth. And as a result, the evangelical community has become a place where people can advocate virtually anything or promote almost any doctrine, and the one thing *no one* is permitted to say is that someone else is wrong.

There's even a name for the new perspective. It's called "the hermeneutic of humility." A syllabus description for a proposed seminary course on the subject says this:

> The course seeks to help students to learn to formulate a new theology and methods that are relevant and meaningful in pluralistic, multicultural, postmodern world in which they are called to minister. It is basically an attempt to articulate a hermeneutic . . . based on dialogue, a sincere effort to go beyond the limits of one's own worldview, that is, *a hermeneutic of humility.*"[2]

Another advocate of the same view says,

> Christians must distill the valuable insights of postmodernism with its multicultural, deconstructed culture. We need to glean from this radical critique what is fitting for a renewed Christian cultural vision— developing *a hermeneutic of humility.* . . . We need to

provide an example of a non-triumphalist, listening, confessing cultural stance.[3]

But the Bible knows nothing of any "hermeneutic" based on a dialogue with other worldviews. Our preaching of Scripture is supposed to be authoritative. In Titus 2:1, the apostle Paul told a young preacher, "But as for you, speak the things which are proper for sound doctrine." At the end of that same chapter, he added, "Speak these things, exhort, and rebuke with all authority. Let no one despise you" (v. 15). The word translated "despise" is the Greek term *kataphroneo*, which literally means, "to think around." Paul is saying to Titus, "Don't let anyone evade you; don't let anyone circumvent the truth. Preach sound doctrine; teach and exhort people with the authority that is inherent in the Word of God, and confront or rebuke people who oppose the truth." In the words of 1 Timothy 4:11: "These things *command* and teach" (emphasis added).

That doesn't mean we're to be abusive or unkind, of

course. It is possible to be both bold and charitable, and that is the balance for which we must strive. Speak the truth in love, Paul says in Ephesians 4:15. But proclaim it nonetheless with *authority*.

There is no other legitimate way to handle biblical truth. It is, after all, truth revealed from God Himself, and it ought to be proclaimed accordingly.

"To the law and to the testimony! If they do not speak according
to this word, it is because there is no light in them."

—ISAIAH 8:20

Scripture says, "No lie is of the truth" (1 John 2:21). As
Christians, we know that whatever contradicts biblical truth is by definition false. In other words, truth is incompatible with error. *Incompatibility* is therefore a fifth essential key word in describing a biblical worldview.

Jesus clearly and unashamedly affirmed the utter exclusivity of Christianity. He said, "I am the way, the truth, and the life. No one comes to the Father except through Me" (John 14:6). "Nor is there salvation in any other, for there is no other name under heaven given among men by which we must be saved" (Acts 4:12). Obviously, that sort of exclusivity is fundamentally incompatible with postmodern tolerance.

As Christians we must understand that whatever opposes God's Word or departs from it in any way is a danger to the very cause of truth. Passivity toward known error is not an option for the Christian. Staunch intolerance of error is built into the very fabric of Scripture. And tolerance of known error is anything but a virtue.

Truth and error cannot be combined to yield something beneficial. They are as incompatible as light and darkness. "What fellowship has righteousness with lawlessness? And what communion has light with darkness? And what accord has Christ with Belial? Or what part has a believer with an unbeliever? And what agreement has the temple of God with idols" (2 Corinthians 6:14–16)?

We can't tell the world, "This is truth, but whatever you want to believe is fine, too." It's *not* fine. Scripture commands us to be *intolerant* of any idea that denies the truth.

Lest anyone misunderstand, I'm not defending dogmatism on any and every theological issue. Some things in Scripture are not perfectly clear. In the words of the Westminster Confession of Faith, "All things in Scripture are not alike plain in themselves, nor alike clear unto all" (1:7). Sometimes we cannot reconstruct the historical context to understand a given passage. One notable example is the mention of "baptism for the dead" in 1 Corinthians 15:29. There are at least forty different views about what that verse means. We cannot be dogmatic about such things. But those are rarities in Scripture.

The central teachings of Scripture are so simple and so clear that even a child can understand. The way of salvation in particular is so clear that "Whoever walks the road, although a fool, shall not go astray" (Isaiah 35:8). In the words of the Westminster Confession again, "Yet those things which are necessary to be known, believed, and observed, for salvation, are so clearly propounded and opened in some place of Scripture or other, that not only the learned, but the unlearned, in a due use of ordinary means, may attain unto a sufficient understanding of them" (1:7).

All the truth that is necessary for our salvation can be easily understood in a true way by anyone who applies common sense and due diligence in seeking to understand what the Bible teaches. And that truth—the core message of Scripture—is incompatible with every other system of belief. We *ought* to be dogmatic about it.

No wonder postmodernism, which prides itself on being tolerant of every competing worldview, is nonetheless hostile to biblical Christianity. Even the most determined postmodernist recognizes that biblical Christianity by its very nature is totally incompatible with a position of uncritical broadmindedness. If we accept the fact that Scripture is the objective, authoritative truth of God, we are bound to see that every other view is *not* equally or potentially valid.

There is no need to seek middle ground through dialogue with proponents of anti-Christian worldviews, as if the truth could be refined by the dialectical method. It is folly to think truth given by divine revelation *needs* any refining or updating. Nor should we imagine that we can meet opposing worldviews on some philosophically neutral ground. The ground between us is not neutral. If we really believe the Word of God is true, we know that everything opposing it is error. And we are to yield no ground whatsoever to error.

In 2 John 9–11 the apostle John wrote, "Whoever transgresses and does not abide in the doctrine of Christ does not have God. . . . If anyone comes to you and does not bring this doctrine, do not receive him into your house nor greet him; for he who greets him shares in his evil deeds." That's incompatibility! Our love for the truth demands an intolerance of error. To be clear, the apostle was not advocating unkindness or inhospitality toward unbelievers in general. (Again, Scripture plainly commands us to show love and kindness even to our enemies.) But John was dealing with the problem of itinerant false teachers in the early church. Typically, those qualified to teach doctrine in that era traveled from city to city and sought shelter in the homes of believers. John was saying that when a known purveyor of false doctrines came seeking such accommodation, he was not to be welcomed into the fellowship; he was not to be offered free housing; he was not to be given encouragement of any type—especially a greeting that signified support for his efforts to teach false doctrines. The antithesis between truth and error was so important that believers were under a bounden duty to make clear their disapproval of everyone who would deliberately corrupt the truth with lies.

Similarly, the apostle Paul wrote, "Even if we, or an angel from heaven, preach any other gospel to you than what we have preached to you, let him be accursed. As we have said before, so now I say again, if anyone preaches any other gospel to you than what you have received, let him be accursed" (Galatians 1:8–9). Strong language, but the point is clear: When someone twists the fundamental truth of the gospel, even if he's an angel or an apostle, let him be cursed.

Warnings against false teachers fill the New Testament. It is a major theme in the pastoral epistles, 2 Peter, Jude, and 2 John. Whatever is unbiblical—including everything untrue, any wrong understanding of Scripture, and all heresy—is not to be tolerated by those who love the truth. It is a danger to the truth and a dishonor to the God of truth. A biblical worldview is incompatible with any kind of tolerance for lies.

> "The integrity of the upright will guide them, But the perversity of
> the unfaithful will destroy them."
>
> —PROVERBS 11:3

$\mathcal{R}$ounding out our list of essential principles for a biblical worldview is the word *integrity*. This flows naturally from all the preceding principles. Since Christianity places such a high premium on truth, we must acknowledge that integrity is an essential virtue, and hypocrisy is a horrible vice.

Integrity is the essential biblical qualification for all ministry. In every list of qualifications for church leaders in the New Testament, one requirement heads the list: The man who would fill any office in the church must be "above reproach" (1 Timothy 3:2, 10; Titus 1:6–7, NASB).

Success in business, skill in public relations, or other earthly talents are not what qualify a man for leadership in the church. The supreme and primary qualification at every level of church leadership is *integrity*—a love for the truth and consistency in living it out practically. To ignore that principle is to sacrifice the premium we place on truth as Christians.

In other words, if we really believe the objective, rationally understood truth of Scripture is both authoritative and incompatible with error, since the Bible is the singular Word of the living God—we must not only preach it; we must live it, too. It is not enough to give lip service. If we genuinely believe the Bible is divine truth, we must allow it to permeate our lives and ministry. To live otherwise is tantamount to denying the truth. People who think otherwise may "profess to know God, but in works they deny Him, being abominable, disobedient, and disqualified for every good work" (Titus 1:16).

Ezra, the high priest in Nehemiah's time, is the prototype of what every godly minister ought to be. "Ezra had prepared his heart to seek the Law of the LORD, *and to do it*, and to teach statutes and ordinances in Israel" (Ezra 7:10, emphasis added).

I learned this lesson from my father, who as a lifelong pastor has been my model of integrity, as was his father before him. I first began to appreciate how difficult the struggle can be when I began in the ministry as a young man in my twenties. I had been in the pastorate for barely a month when I was asked to perform a wedding for a girl in our church who was planning to marry an unbeliever. In a meeting of the church board, some of the leaders urged me to do the wedding because the girl's father was an influential man. A lot was at stake, they said. We might lose this family from the church if I declined.

I said, "But I can't do that. I can't do what Scripture clearly forbids. Believers are not to be unequally yoked with unbelievers. Second Corinthians 6:14."

They were already prepared for that. They replied, "Well, OK. We understand your feelings. We know a minister from somewhere else who will come in and do it, so that this girl can be married in the church."

I asked them, "But whose church is this? Is this *your* church to be used at your discretion, or is this *Christ's* church?"

They replied to their great credit, "You're right; we can't do it. This is Christ's church."

That was the Rubicon for Grace Community Church. That was the moment when the future of our congregation was decided. Yes, an entire family left, and several other people withdrew their membership over that incident as well. But we decided as elders that day that we would not only *preach* the Word of God; we would expect it to be *lived out* in the corporate life of the church.

That sort of obedience to the Word of God has shaped and molded our ministry over the years. It shows up even in the way we worship. We don't entertain people. We don't have a dog-and-pony show. We gather to worship God, to exalt Christ, and to hear the Word of God preached. We practice church discipline as outlined in Matthew 18:15–20. We seek to obey what Scripture teaches, no matter how politically incorrect or out of fashion it might seem. And at a time when many churches are becoming more and more like the world, our goal is to be conformed more and more to the standard set forth in the Scriptures. God has blessed that, and I am convinced it is because our elders have sought to uphold the standard of biblical integrity at every level of leadership.

Unfortunately, the evangelical movement today is drifting from these fundamental principles and has already begun to embrace postmodern ideas uncritically. Evangelicalism is losing its footing; people's confidence in the Scriptures is eroding; and the church is losing its testimony. Fewer and fewer Christians are willing to stand against the trends of this generation, and the effects have been disastrous. Subjectivity, irrationality, worldliness, uncertainty, compromise, and hypocrisy have already become commonplace among churches and organizations that once constituted the evangelical mainstream.

The only cure, I am convinced, is a conscious, wholesale rejection of postmodern values and a return to these six distinctives of biblical Christianity. We must be faithful to guard the treasure of truth that has been entrusted to us (2 Timothy 1:14). If we do not, who will?

Endnotes

CHAPTER 1: THE CHURCH VS. THE WORLD

1. See, for example, www.religioustolerance.org.

CHAPTER 2: OBJECTIVITY

1. A transcript of Clinton's November 7, 2001, speech was pro-
    vided by the Georgetown University Office of Protocol and
    Events. (The transcript is available on the World Wide Web
    at http://www.georgetown.edu/admin/publicaffairs/proto-
    col_events/events/clinton_glf110701.htm).

CHAPTER 3: RATIONALITY

1. For a more in-depth treatment of neo-orthodoxy and irra-
    tionalism, see John MacArthur, *Reckless Faith* (Wheaton, IL:
    Crossway, 1994), 25–30.

CHAPTER 5: AUTHORITY

1. Sean D. Hamill, "Willow Creek welcomes Muslim cleric's perspective; Pastor, *imam* have dialogue at suburban church," *Chicago Tribune*, October 12, 2001.
2. Stephen S. Kim, Ph.D., "Science and Theology in Dialogue: A Hermeneutic of Humility," Claremont School of Theology. (Syllabus On the World Wide Web at: http://www.templeton.org/pdf/SandR/kim.pdf). Emphasis added.
3. Bruce Herman, "Toward a Culture of Hope: Facing Christ in the Fact of the Other," from a lecture delivered August 6, 2001, at the Glen Workshop in Santa Fe, New Mexico, sponsored by *Image: A Journal of the Arts and Religion*. Emphasis added.